50 Unique Ways to Cook with Quinoa

By: Kelly Johnson

Table of Contents

- Quinoa Salad with Roasted Vegetables
- Quinoa and Black Bean Tacos
- Quinoa Stuffed Bell Peppers
- Quinoa Breakfast Bowl with Berries and Nuts
- Quinoa and Spinach Frittata
- Quinoa and Chickpea Buddha Bowl
- Quinoa and Avocado Sushi Rolls
- Quinoa Fried Rice
- Quinoa and Vegetable Stir-Fry
- Quinoa and Lentil Soup
- Quinoa and Apple Breakfast Muffins
- Quinoa Pizza Crust
- Quinoa and Mango Salad
- Quinoa Energy Bars
- Quinoa and Shrimp Paella
- Quinoa Chili
- Quinoa and Zucchini Cakes
- Quinoa Tabouli Salad
- Quinoa and Cauliflower Curry
- Quinoa Porridge with Coconut Milk
- Quinoa and Egg Breakfast Casserole
- Quinoa and Sweet Potato Hash
- Quinoa Risotto with Mushrooms
- Quinoa and Roasted Beet Salad
- Quinoa Burgers
- Quinoa and Coconut Macaroons
- Quinoa Stuffed Acorn Squash
- Quinoa and Pomegranate Salad
- Quinoa Pasta Salad
- Quinoa and Chicken Stir-Fry
- Quinoa and Kale Soup
- Quinoa and Almond Joy Smoothie
- Quinoa and Roasted Carrot Salad
- Quinoa and Herb Crusted Fish
- Quinoa Granola

- Quinoa and Grilled Vegetable Skewers
- Quinoa Pancakes
- Quinoa and Nut Butter Energy Bites
- Quinoa and Cabbage Slaw
- Quinoa and Lemon Garlic Roasted Broccoli
- Quinoa and Turkey Stuffed Zucchini
- Quinoa Chocolate Chip Cookies
- Quinoa and Blueberry Smoothie Bowl
- Quinoa and Feta Stuffed Tomatoes
- Quinoa and Green Bean Salad
- Quinoa and Herb Flatbread
- Quinoa and Beef Stir-Fry
- Quinoa and Peach Salad
- Quinoa and Vegetable Curry
- Quinoa and Chia Seed Pudding

Quinoa Salad with Roasted Vegetables

Ingredients:

- 1 cup quinoa, cooked
- 2 cups assorted vegetables (e.g., bell peppers, zucchini, carrots), diced
- 3 tablespoons olive oil
- 1 teaspoon dried oregano
- Salt and pepper, to taste
- 1/4 cup feta cheese, crumbled (optional)
- Fresh parsley, chopped for garnish

Instructions:

1. Preheat the oven to 425°F (220°C). Toss the diced vegetables with olive oil, oregano, salt, and pepper on a baking sheet. Roast for 20-25 minutes until tender.
2. In a large bowl, combine cooked quinoa and roasted vegetables.
3. If using, add feta cheese and toss gently. Garnish with parsley and serve warm or at room temperature.

Quinoa and Black Bean Tacos

Ingredients:

- 1 cup quinoa, cooked
- 1 can (15 oz) black beans, rinsed and drained
- 1 teaspoon cumin
- 1 teaspoon chili powder
- Salt and pepper, to taste
- Corn tortillas
- Toppings: avocado, salsa, cilantro, lime

Instructions:

1. In a skillet, combine cooked quinoa, black beans, cumin, chili powder, salt, and pepper. Cook over medium heat until heated through.
2. Warm corn tortillas in a separate skillet.
3. Fill each tortilla with the quinoa and black bean mixture and top with avocado, salsa, cilantro, and a squeeze of lime.

Quinoa Stuffed Bell Peppers

Ingredients:

- 4 bell peppers, halved and seeds removed
- 1 cup quinoa, cooked
- 1 can (15 oz) diced tomatoes, drained
- 1/2 cup corn (fresh or frozen)
- 1 teaspoon cumin
- Salt and pepper, to taste
- 1/2 cup shredded cheese (optional)

Instructions:

1. Preheat the oven to 375°F (190°C).
2. In a bowl, mix cooked quinoa, diced tomatoes, corn, cumin, salt, and pepper.
3. Stuff the halved bell peppers with the quinoa mixture and place in a baking dish.
4. If desired, sprinkle cheese on top. Cover with foil and bake for 30-35 minutes until the peppers are tender.

Quinoa Breakfast Bowl with Berries and Nuts

Ingredients:

- 1 cup quinoa, cooked
- 1 cup mixed berries (fresh or frozen)
- 1/4 cup nuts (e.g., almonds, walnuts), chopped
- 1 tablespoon honey or maple syrup (optional)
- 1/2 teaspoon cinnamon

Instructions:

1. In a bowl, combine cooked quinoa, mixed berries, nuts, honey or maple syrup, and cinnamon.
2. Serve warm or chilled as a healthy breakfast option.

Quinoa and Spinach Frittata

Ingredients:

- 1 cup quinoa, cooked
- 4 large eggs
- 2 cups fresh spinach
- 1/2 cup feta cheese, crumbled
- Salt and pepper, to taste
- Olive oil for cooking

Instructions:

1. Preheat the oven to 350°F (175°C).
2. In a skillet, sauté spinach in olive oil until wilted.
3. In a bowl, whisk eggs, then mix in cooked quinoa, sautéed spinach, feta, salt, and pepper.
4. Pour the mixture into a greased oven-safe skillet and bake for 25-30 minutes until set.

Quinoa and Chickpea Buddha Bowl

Ingredients:

- 1 cup quinoa, cooked
- 1 can (15 oz) chickpeas, rinsed and drained
- 1 cup mixed greens
- 1/2 avocado, sliced
- 1/2 cucumber, diced
- Tahini dressing (for drizzling)
- Salt and pepper, to taste

Instructions:

1. In a bowl, layer cooked quinoa, chickpeas, mixed greens, avocado, and cucumber.
2. Drizzle with tahini dressing and season with salt and pepper. Serve chilled or at room temperature.

Quinoa and Avocado Sushi Rolls

Ingredients:

- 1 cup quinoa, cooked and cooled
- 4 sheets nori (seaweed)
- 1 avocado, sliced
- 1 cucumber, julienned
- Soy sauce for dipping

Instructions:

1. Place a sheet of nori on a bamboo sushi mat. Spread a thin layer of quinoa evenly over the nori.
2. Arrange avocado and cucumber slices on top of the quinoa.
3. Roll the sushi tightly using the mat, then slice into pieces. Serve with soy sauce for dipping.

Quinoa Fried Rice

Ingredients:

- 1 cup quinoa, cooked
- 2 cups mixed vegetables (e.g., peas, carrots, bell peppers)
- 2 eggs, beaten
- 3 tablespoons soy sauce
- 2 green onions, sliced
- Olive oil for cooking

Instructions:

1. In a skillet, heat olive oil over medium heat. Add mixed vegetables and sauté until tender.
2. Push the vegetables to one side of the skillet and pour in beaten eggs, scrambling them until cooked.
3. Add cooked quinoa and soy sauce, stirring to combine everything. Garnish with green onions before serving.

Quinoa and Vegetable Stir-Fry

Ingredients:

- 1 cup quinoa, cooked
- 2 cups mixed vegetables (e.g., bell peppers, broccoli, carrots)
- 3 tablespoons soy sauce
- 1 tablespoon sesame oil
- 2 cloves garlic, minced
- 1 teaspoon ginger, minced
- Sesame seeds for garnish

Instructions:

1. Heat sesame oil in a large skillet over medium heat. Add garlic and ginger, sautéing until fragrant.
2. Add mixed vegetables and stir-fry until tender.
3. Stir in cooked quinoa and soy sauce, cooking for an additional 2-3 minutes.
4. Garnish with sesame seeds before serving.

Quinoa and Lentil Soup

Ingredients:

- 1 cup quinoa, rinsed
- 1 cup lentils, rinsed
- 1 onion, chopped
- 2 carrots, diced
- 2 celery stalks, diced
- 4 cups vegetable broth
- 1 can (14 oz) diced tomatoes
- 2 teaspoons cumin
- Salt and pepper, to taste
- Olive oil for cooking

Instructions:

1. In a large pot, heat olive oil over medium heat. Add onion, carrots, and celery, cooking until softened.
2. Stir in quinoa, lentils, broth, diced tomatoes, cumin, salt, and pepper.
3. Bring to a boil, then reduce heat and simmer for 30-35 minutes until lentils and quinoa are tender.

Quinoa and Apple Breakfast Muffins

Ingredients:

- 1 cup cooked quinoa
- 1 cup whole wheat flour
- 1/2 cup applesauce
- 1/2 cup honey or maple syrup
- 2 eggs
- 1 teaspoon cinnamon
- 1/2 teaspoon baking powder
- 1/2 teaspoon baking soda
- 1 apple, diced

Instructions:

1. Preheat the oven to 350°F (175°C) and line a muffin tin with liners.
2. In a bowl, mix cooked quinoa, flour, applesauce, honey, eggs, cinnamon, baking powder, and baking soda until well combined.
3. Fold in diced apple.
4. Fill muffin tins and bake for 20-25 minutes or until a toothpick comes out clean.

Quinoa Pizza Crust

Ingredients:

- 1 cup cooked quinoa
- 1/2 cup almond flour
- 1/4 cup ground flaxseed
- 1 teaspoon Italian seasoning
- 1/2 teaspoon garlic powder
- Salt, to taste
- 1/4 cup water

Instructions:

1. Preheat the oven to 425°F (220°C) and line a baking sheet with parchment paper.
2. In a bowl, combine cooked quinoa, almond flour, ground flaxseed, Italian seasoning, garlic powder, salt, and water until a dough forms.
3. Spread the dough into a circular shape on the baking sheet.
4. Bake for 15-20 minutes until the edges are golden. Top with your favorite pizza toppings and return to the oven until heated through.

Quinoa and Mango Salad

Ingredients:

- 1 cup cooked quinoa, cooled
- 1 ripe mango, diced
- 1/2 red bell pepper, diced
- 1/4 red onion, finely chopped
- 1/4 cup cilantro, chopped
- Juice of 1 lime
- Salt and pepper, to taste

Instructions:

1. In a large bowl, combine cooked quinoa, mango, bell pepper, red onion, and cilantro.
2. Drizzle with lime juice and season with salt and pepper. Toss gently to combine and serve chilled.

Quinoa Energy Bars

Ingredients:

- 1 cup cooked quinoa
- 1 cup oats
- 1/2 cup almond butter
- 1/2 cup honey or maple syrup
- 1/2 cup dried fruit (e.g., cranberries, raisins)
- 1/4 cup nuts or seeds (e.g., almonds, chia seeds)
- 1 teaspoon vanilla extract

Instructions:

1. Preheat the oven to 350°F (175°C) and line an 8x8 inch baking dish with parchment paper.
2. In a bowl, mix all ingredients until well combined.
3. Press the mixture into the prepared baking dish.
4. Bake for 20-25 minutes until set. Allow to cool before cutting into bars.

Quinoa and Shrimp Paella

Ingredients:

- 1 cup quinoa, rinsed
- 1 pound shrimp, peeled and deveined
- 1 onion, chopped
- 2 cloves garlic, minced
- 1 red bell pepper, diced
- 1 can (14 oz) diced tomatoes
- 2 cups vegetable broth
- 1 teaspoon smoked paprika
- 1/2 teaspoon saffron (optional)
- Olive oil for cooking

Instructions:

1. In a large skillet, heat olive oil over medium heat. Add onion, garlic, and bell pepper, sautéing until soft.
2. Stir in quinoa, tomatoes, broth, smoked paprika, and saffron. Bring to a boil.
3. Reduce heat and simmer for 15 minutes, then add shrimp. Cook until shrimp are pink and quinoa is tender.

Quinoa Chili

Ingredients:

- 1 cup quinoa, rinsed
- 1 can (15 oz) kidney beans, rinsed and drained
- 1 can (15 oz) black beans, rinsed and drained
- 1 can (14 oz) diced tomatoes
- 1 onion, chopped
- 2 cloves garlic, minced
- 2 tablespoons chili powder
- 1 teaspoon cumin
- Salt and pepper, to taste
- Olive oil for cooking

Instructions:

1. In a large pot, heat olive oil over medium heat. Add onion and garlic, cooking until softened.
2. Stir in quinoa, kidney beans, black beans, diced tomatoes, chili powder, cumin, salt, and pepper.
3. Add 4 cups of water, bring to a boil, then reduce heat and simmer for 30 minutes until quinoa is cooked.

Quinoa and Zucchini Cakes

Ingredients:

- 1 cup cooked quinoa
- 2 medium zucchinis, grated
- 1/2 cup breadcrumbs
- 1/4 cup grated Parmesan cheese
- 2 eggs, beaten
- 2 cloves garlic, minced
- Salt and pepper, to taste
- Olive oil for frying

Instructions:

1. In a large bowl, combine cooked quinoa, grated zucchini, breadcrumbs, Parmesan cheese, beaten eggs, garlic, salt, and pepper.
2. Mix until well combined and form into patties.
3. Heat olive oil in a skillet over medium heat and fry the patties for about 3-4 minutes on each side until golden brown.
4. Serve warm with a dipping sauce or salad.

Quinoa Tabouli Salad

Ingredients:

- 1 cup cooked quinoa, cooled
- 1/2 cup parsley, finely chopped
- 1/4 cup mint, finely chopped
- 1 tomato, diced
- 1 cucumber, diced
- Juice of 1 lemon
- 2 tablespoons olive oil
- Salt and pepper, to taste

Instructions:

1. In a large bowl, combine cooked quinoa, parsley, mint, tomato, and cucumber.
2. Drizzle with lemon juice and olive oil, then season with salt and pepper.
3. Toss gently to combine and serve chilled.

Quinoa and Cauliflower Curry

Ingredients:

- 1 cup quinoa, rinsed
- 1 head cauliflower, cut into florets
- 1 onion, chopped
- 2 cloves garlic, minced
- 1 tablespoon curry powder
- 1 can (14 oz) coconut milk
- 2 cups vegetable broth
- Olive oil for cooking

Instructions:

1. In a large pot, heat olive oil over medium heat. Add onion and garlic, cooking until softened.
2. Stir in curry powder and cook for an additional minute.
3. Add cauliflower, quinoa, coconut milk, and vegetable broth. Bring to a boil, then reduce heat and simmer for 20-25 minutes until quinoa and cauliflower are tender.

Quinoa Porridge with Coconut Milk

Ingredients:

- 1 cup cooked quinoa
- 1 cup coconut milk
- 1 tablespoon honey or maple syrup
- 1/2 teaspoon vanilla extract
- Fresh fruits and nuts for topping

Instructions:

1. In a saucepan, combine cooked quinoa, coconut milk, honey, and vanilla extract.
2. Heat over medium heat, stirring until warmed through.
3. Serve topped with fresh fruits and nuts.

Quinoa and Egg Breakfast Casserole

Ingredients:

- 1 cup cooked quinoa
- 6 eggs
- 1 cup spinach, chopped
- 1/2 cup bell pepper, diced
- 1/2 cup cheese (e.g., cheddar or feta)
- Salt and pepper, to taste

Instructions:

1. Preheat the oven to 350°F (175°C) and grease a baking dish.
2. In a bowl, whisk together eggs, salt, and pepper.
3. Stir in cooked quinoa, spinach, bell pepper, and cheese.
4. Pour the mixture into the baking dish and bake for 25-30 minutes until set and golden.

Quinoa and Sweet Potato Hash

Ingredients:

- 1 cup cooked quinoa
- 1 medium sweet potato, diced
- 1 bell pepper, diced
- 1 onion, diced
- 2 tablespoons olive oil
- Salt and pepper, to taste
- Fresh herbs for garnish

Instructions:

1. In a large skillet, heat olive oil over medium heat. Add sweet potato and cook until tender.
2. Stir in onion and bell pepper, cooking until softened.
3. Add cooked quinoa, season with salt and pepper, and mix well.
4. Cook for an additional 5 minutes, garnish with fresh herbs, and serve warm.

Quinoa Risotto with Mushrooms

Ingredients:

- 1 cup quinoa, rinsed
- 1 cup mushrooms, sliced
- 1 onion, chopped
- 2 cloves garlic, minced
- 4 cups vegetable broth
- 1/2 cup Parmesan cheese (optional)
- Olive oil for cooking

Instructions:

1. In a pot, heat olive oil over medium heat. Add onion and garlic, cooking until softened.
2. Stir in mushrooms and cook until they release moisture.
3. Add quinoa and gradually add vegetable broth, one cup at a time, stirring frequently until absorbed.
4. Stir in Parmesan cheese if using, and serve warm.

Quinoa and Roasted Beet Salad

Ingredients:

- 1 cup cooked quinoa, cooled
- 2 cups roasted beets, diced
- 1/4 cup feta cheese, crumbled
- 1/4 cup walnuts, chopped
- 2 tablespoons balsamic vinegar
- 2 tablespoons olive oil
- Salt and pepper, to taste

Instructions:

1. In a large bowl, combine cooked quinoa, roasted beets, feta cheese, and walnuts.
2. Drizzle with balsamic vinegar and olive oil, then season with salt and pepper.
3. Toss gently to combine and serve chilled.

Quinoa Burgers

Ingredients:

- 1 cup cooked quinoa
- 1/2 cup breadcrumbs
- 1/2 cup black beans, mashed
- 1/4 cup chopped onion
- 1/4 cup chopped bell pepper
- 1 egg, beaten
- 1 teaspoon cumin
- Salt and pepper, to taste
- Olive oil for frying

Instructions:

1. In a bowl, mix cooked quinoa, breadcrumbs, black beans, onion, bell pepper, beaten egg, cumin, salt, and pepper until well combined.
2. Form the mixture into patties.
3. Heat olive oil in a skillet over medium heat and cook the patties for about 5 minutes on each side until golden brown.
4. Serve on buns or with salad.

Quinoa and Coconut Macaroons

Ingredients:

- 2 cups shredded coconut
- 1/2 cup cooked quinoa
- 1/2 cup sweetened condensed milk
- 1 teaspoon vanilla extract
- Pinch of salt

Instructions:

1. Preheat the oven to 350°F (175°C) and line a baking sheet with parchment paper.
2. In a bowl, mix shredded coconut, cooked quinoa, condensed milk, vanilla extract, and salt until combined.
3. Drop spoonfuls of the mixture onto the prepared baking sheet.
4. Bake for 15-20 minutes until golden. Let cool before serving.

Quinoa Stuffed Acorn Squash

Ingredients:

- 2 acorn squashes, halved and seeds removed
- 1 cup cooked quinoa
- 1/2 cup cranberries
- 1/2 cup walnuts, chopped
- 1/2 teaspoon cinnamon
- Salt and pepper, to taste
- Olive oil for drizzling

Instructions:

1. Preheat the oven to 400°F (200°C).
2. Place acorn squash halves cut side up on a baking sheet, drizzle with olive oil, and season with salt and pepper.
3. Roast for 25-30 minutes until tender.
4. In a bowl, mix cooked quinoa, cranberries, walnuts, cinnamon, salt, and pepper.
5. Fill each squash half with the quinoa mixture and return to the oven for 10 minutes. Serve warm.

Quinoa and Pomegranate Salad

Ingredients:

- 1 cup cooked quinoa, cooled
- 1 cup pomegranate seeds
- 1/2 cup chopped cucumber
- 1/4 cup chopped red onion
- 1/4 cup feta cheese, crumbled
- 2 tablespoons olive oil
- Juice of 1 lemon
- Salt and pepper, to taste

Instructions:

1. In a large bowl, combine cooked quinoa, pomegranate seeds, cucumber, red onion, and feta cheese.
2. Drizzle with olive oil and lemon juice, then season with salt and pepper.
3. Toss gently to combine and serve chilled.

Quinoa Pasta Salad

Ingredients:

- 1 cup cooked quinoa
- 8 oz cooked pasta (e.g., rotini or penne)
- 1 cup cherry tomatoes, halved
- 1/2 cup olives, sliced
- 1/4 cup diced bell pepper
- 1/4 cup Italian dressing

Instructions:

1. In a large bowl, combine cooked quinoa, cooked pasta, cherry tomatoes, olives, and bell pepper.
2. Drizzle with Italian dressing and toss to combine.
3. Serve chilled or at room temperature.

Quinoa and Chicken Stir-Fry

Ingredients:

- 1 cup cooked quinoa
- 1 cup cooked chicken, diced
- 2 cups mixed vegetables (e.g., bell peppers, broccoli, carrots)
- 2 tablespoons soy sauce
- 1 tablespoon sesame oil
- 2 cloves garlic, minced
- 1 tablespoon ginger, grated

Instructions:

1. In a large skillet, heat sesame oil over medium heat. Add garlic and ginger, cooking until fragrant.
2. Add mixed vegetables and stir-fry until tender.
3. Stir in cooked chicken and quinoa, then add soy sauce. Cook for an additional 5 minutes until heated through.

Quinoa and Kale Soup

Ingredients:

- 1 cup cooked quinoa
- 4 cups vegetable broth
- 2 cups kale, chopped
- 1 cup diced tomatoes
- 1 onion, chopped
- 2 cloves garlic, minced
- 1 teaspoon thyme
- Salt and pepper, to taste

Instructions:

1. In a large pot, sauté onion and garlic until softened.
2. Add vegetable broth, kale, diced tomatoes, thyme, salt, and pepper. Bring to a boil.
3. Reduce heat and simmer for 15 minutes. Stir in cooked quinoa and heat through before serving.

Quinoa and Almond Joy Smoothie

Ingredients:

- 1/2 cup cooked quinoa
- 1 banana
- 1 cup almond milk
- 1 tablespoon almond butter
- 1 tablespoon cocoa powder
- 1 tablespoon honey (optional)
- Ice cubes

Instructions:

1. In a blender, combine cooked quinoa, banana, almond milk, almond butter, cocoa powder, honey, and ice cubes.
2. Blend until smooth and creamy.
3. Serve chilled in a glass.

Quinoa and Roasted Carrot Salad

Ingredients:

- 1 cup cooked quinoa
- 4 large carrots, sliced
- 2 tablespoons olive oil
- Salt and pepper, to taste
- 1/4 cup chopped parsley
- 1/4 cup feta cheese (optional)
- 1 tablespoon balsamic vinegar

Instructions:

1. Preheat the oven to 400°F (200°C).
2. Toss sliced carrots with olive oil, salt, and pepper, and spread them on a baking sheet. Roast for 20-25 minutes until tender.
3. In a bowl, combine cooked quinoa, roasted carrots, parsley, and feta cheese.
4. Drizzle with balsamic vinegar, toss to combine, and serve warm or at room temperature.

Quinoa and Herb Crusted Fish

Ingredients:

- 4 fish fillets (e.g., cod, tilapia)
- 1 cup cooked quinoa
- 1/2 cup breadcrumbs
- 1/4 cup chopped fresh herbs (e.g., parsley, dill)
- 1 egg, beaten
- Salt and pepper, to taste
- Olive oil for drizzling

Instructions:

1. Preheat the oven to 375°F (190°C) and line a baking sheet with parchment paper.
2. In a bowl, mix cooked quinoa, breadcrumbs, herbs, beaten egg, salt, and pepper.
3. Press the mixture onto the fish fillets and place them on the baking sheet.
4. Drizzle with olive oil and bake for 15-20 minutes until the fish is cooked through and the crust is golden.

Quinoa Granola

Ingredients:

- 2 cups rolled oats
- 1 cup cooked quinoa
- 1/2 cup nuts (e.g., almonds, walnuts)
- 1/2 cup honey or maple syrup
- 1/4 cup coconut oil, melted
- 1 teaspoon vanilla extract
- 1 teaspoon cinnamon
- 1/2 cup dried fruits (optional)

Instructions:

1. Preheat the oven to 350°F (175°C) and line a baking sheet with parchment paper.
2. In a large bowl, mix oats, cooked quinoa, nuts, honey, melted coconut oil, vanilla, and cinnamon.
3. Spread the mixture evenly on the baking sheet and bake for 20-25 minutes, stirring halfway through.
4. Let cool and stir in dried fruits before storing in an airtight container.

Quinoa and Grilled Vegetable Skewers

Ingredients:

- 1 cup cooked quinoa
- 2 bell peppers, chopped
- 1 zucchini, sliced
- 1 red onion, cut into chunks
- 1 cup cherry tomatoes
- 2 tablespoons olive oil
- Salt and pepper, to taste
- Skewers

Instructions:

1. Preheat the grill to medium-high heat.
2. In a bowl, toss vegetables with olive oil, salt, and pepper.
3. Thread the vegetables onto skewers, alternating types.
4. Grill skewers for 10-15 minutes, turning occasionally until vegetables are tender. Serve with cooked quinoa.

Quinoa Pancakes

Ingredients:

- 1 cup cooked quinoa
- 1 cup flour (whole wheat or all-purpose)
- 1 cup milk (or non-dairy alternative)
- 1 egg
- 1 tablespoon baking powder
- 1 teaspoon vanilla extract
- 1/2 teaspoon salt

Instructions:

1. In a bowl, combine cooked quinoa, flour, milk, egg, baking powder, vanilla, and salt. Mix until smooth.
2. Heat a non-stick skillet over medium heat and pour 1/4 cup of batter for each pancake.
3. Cook until bubbles form on the surface, then flip and cook until golden.
4. Serve warm with syrup or fresh fruit.

Quinoa and Nut Butter Energy Bites

Ingredients:

- 1 cup cooked quinoa
- 1/2 cup nut butter (e.g., almond or peanut)
- 1/4 cup honey or maple syrup
- 1/2 cup oats
- 1/4 cup chocolate chips (optional)
- 1/4 cup chopped nuts or seeds

Instructions:

1. In a bowl, mix cooked quinoa, nut butter, honey, oats, chocolate chips, and nuts until well combined.
2. Refrigerate the mixture for about 30 minutes to firm up.
3. Roll into small balls and store in an airtight container in the fridge.

Quinoa and Cabbage Slaw

Ingredients:

- 1 cup cooked quinoa
- 2 cups green cabbage, shredded
- 1 carrot, grated
- 1/4 cup chopped green onions
- 1/4 cup apple cider vinegar
- 2 tablespoons olive oil
- Salt and pepper, to taste

Instructions:

1. In a large bowl, combine cooked quinoa, shredded cabbage, grated carrot, and green onions.
2. In a small bowl, whisk together apple cider vinegar, olive oil, salt, and pepper.
3. Pour the dressing over the salad and toss to combine. Serve chilled.

Quinoa and Lemon Garlic Roasted Broccoli

Ingredients:

- 1 head broccoli, cut into florets
- 2 tablespoons olive oil
- 3 cloves garlic, minced
- Juice of 1 lemon
- 1 cup cooked quinoa
- Salt and pepper, to taste

Instructions:

1. Preheat the oven to 425°F (220°C).
2. In a bowl, toss broccoli florets with olive oil, garlic, salt, and pepper.
3. Spread broccoli on a baking sheet and roast for 20-25 minutes until tender.
4. Toss roasted broccoli with cooked quinoa and lemon juice before serving.

Quinoa and Turkey Stuffed Zucchini

Ingredients:

- 4 medium zucchinis, halved lengthwise
- 1 cup cooked quinoa
- 1 pound ground turkey
- 1 cup diced tomatoes (canned or fresh)
- 1 teaspoon Italian seasoning
- Salt and pepper, to taste
- 1/2 cup shredded mozzarella cheese

Instructions:

1. Preheat the oven to 375°F (190°C) and grease a baking dish.
2. In a skillet, cook ground turkey over medium heat until browned. Drain excess fat.
3. Stir in cooked quinoa, diced tomatoes, Italian seasoning, salt, and pepper.
4. Scoop the mixture into zucchini halves and place in the baking dish.
5. Top with shredded mozzarella cheese and bake for 25-30 minutes until zucchinis are tender.

Quinoa Chocolate Chip Cookies

Ingredients:

- 1 cup cooked quinoa
- 1 cup almond flour
- 1/2 cup coconut sugar or brown sugar
- 1/4 cup coconut oil, melted
- 1/2 teaspoon vanilla extract
- 1/2 teaspoon baking soda
- 1/4 teaspoon salt
- 1/2 cup chocolate chips

Instructions:

1. Preheat the oven to 350°F (175°C) and line a baking sheet with parchment paper.
2. In a bowl, mix cooked quinoa, almond flour, coconut sugar, melted coconut oil, vanilla, baking soda, and salt until combined.
3. Fold in chocolate chips.
4. Scoop tablespoon-sized balls of dough onto the baking sheet and flatten slightly.
5. Bake for 12-15 minutes until edges are golden. Let cool before serving.

Quinoa and Blueberry Smoothie Bowl

Ingredients:

- 1 cup cooked quinoa
- 1 banana
- 1 cup almond milk (or milk of choice)
- 1/2 cup blueberries (fresh or frozen)
- 1 tablespoon honey or maple syrup (optional)
- Toppings: sliced fruit, nuts, seeds, granola

Instructions:

1. In a blender, combine cooked quinoa, banana, almond milk, blueberries, and sweetener (if using). Blend until smooth.
2. Pour the smoothie into a bowl and top with your choice of sliced fruit, nuts, seeds, or granola. Serve immediately.

Quinoa and Feta Stuffed Tomatoes

Ingredients:

- 4 large tomatoes
- 1 cup cooked quinoa
- 1/2 cup feta cheese, crumbled
- 1/4 cup fresh basil, chopped
- 1 tablespoon olive oil
- Salt and pepper, to taste

Instructions:

1. Preheat the oven to 375°F (190°C) and grease a baking dish.
2. Cut the tops off the tomatoes and scoop out the insides.
3. In a bowl, combine cooked quinoa, feta cheese, basil, olive oil, salt, and pepper.
4. Stuff the mixture into the hollowed tomatoes and place them in the baking dish.
5. Bake for 25-30 minutes until tomatoes are tender and filling is heated through.

Quinoa and Green Bean Salad

Ingredients:

- 1 cup cooked quinoa
- 1 cup green beans, trimmed and blanched
- 1/2 cup cherry tomatoes, halved
- 1/4 cup red onion, finely chopped
- 1/4 cup feta cheese (optional)
- 2 tablespoons olive oil
- 1 tablespoon lemon juice
- Salt and pepper, to taste

Instructions:

1. In a large bowl, combine cooked quinoa, green beans, cherry tomatoes, red onion, and feta cheese (if using).
2. In a small bowl, whisk together olive oil, lemon juice, salt, and pepper.
3. Drizzle the dressing over the salad and toss to combine. Serve chilled or at room temperature.

Quinoa and Herb Flatbread

Ingredients:

- 1 cup cooked quinoa
- 1 cup whole wheat flour
- 1/2 cup water
- 1 tablespoon olive oil
- 1 teaspoon baking powder
- 1 teaspoon dried herbs (e.g., oregano, thyme)
- Salt, to taste

Instructions:

1. In a bowl, mix cooked quinoa, whole wheat flour, water, olive oil, baking powder, dried herbs, and salt until a dough forms.
2. Divide the dough into small balls and roll out each ball into a flatbread shape.
3. Heat a skillet over medium heat and cook each flatbread for 2-3 minutes on each side until lightly browned.
4. Serve warm as a side or wrap with your favorite fillings.

Quinoa and Beef Stir-Fry

Ingredients:

- 1 cup cooked quinoa
- 1 pound beef (sirloin or flank), thinly sliced
- 2 cups mixed vegetables (bell peppers, broccoli, carrots)
- 3 tablespoons soy sauce
- 2 tablespoons sesame oil
- 1 tablespoon ginger, minced
- 2 garlic cloves, minced
- Salt and pepper, to taste
- Green onions, sliced (for garnish)

Instructions:

1. In a large skillet or wok, heat sesame oil over medium-high heat.
2. Add minced ginger and garlic, sauté for about 30 seconds.
3. Add sliced beef and cook until browned.
4. Stir in mixed vegetables and cook until tender-crisp.
5. Add cooked quinoa and soy sauce, stirring to combine.
6. Season with salt and pepper. Serve hot, garnished with green onions.

Quinoa and Peach Salad

Ingredients:

- 1 cup cooked quinoa
- 2 ripe peaches, sliced
- 1 cup arugula or spinach
- 1/4 cup feta cheese, crumbled
- 1/4 cup walnuts, chopped
- 2 tablespoons balsamic vinegar
- 1 tablespoon olive oil
- Salt and pepper, to taste

Instructions:

1. In a large bowl, combine cooked quinoa, sliced peaches, arugula, feta cheese, and walnuts.
2. In a small bowl, whisk together balsamic vinegar, olive oil, salt, and pepper.
3. Drizzle the dressing over the salad and toss gently to combine. Serve immediately.

Quinoa and Vegetable Curry

Ingredients:

- 1 cup cooked quinoa
- 1 tablespoon coconut oil
- 1 onion, chopped
- 2 garlic cloves, minced
- 1 tablespoon ginger, minced
- 2 cups mixed vegetables (e.g., bell peppers, carrots, peas)
- 1 can (14 oz) coconut milk
- 2 tablespoons curry powder
- Salt, to taste
- Fresh cilantro (for garnish)

Instructions:

1. In a large pot, heat coconut oil over medium heat.
2. Add chopped onion, garlic, and ginger; sauté until onion is translucent.
3. Stir in mixed vegetables and curry powder, cooking for another 5 minutes.
4. Pour in coconut milk and bring to a simmer.
5. Add cooked quinoa and salt, stirring to combine.
6. Cook for another 5-10 minutes. Serve hot, garnished with fresh cilantro.

Quinoa and Chia Seed Pudding

Ingredients:

- 1/2 cup quinoa, rinsed and cooked
- 1/4 cup chia seeds
- 2 cups almond milk (or any milk of choice)
- 2 tablespoons maple syrup or honey
- 1 teaspoon vanilla extract
- Fresh fruits and nuts (for topping)

Instructions:

1. In a bowl, whisk together cooked quinoa, chia seeds, almond milk, maple syrup, and vanilla extract.
2. Refrigerate for at least 2 hours or overnight until thickened.
3. Serve in bowls topped with fresh fruits and nuts.

www.ingramcontent.com/pod-product-compliance
Lightning Source LLC
LaVergne TN
LVHW081506060526
838201LV00056BA/2970